T0206824

Letters to Self

Translated from the Gujarati by
BHAWANA SOMAAYA

Narendra Modi

FiNGERPRINT!

Published by

FiNGERPRINT!

An imprint of Prakash Books India Pvt. Ltd.

113/A, Darya Ganj, New Delhi-110 002,
Tel: (011) 2324 7062 – 65, Fax: (011) 2324 6975
Email: info@prakashbooks.com/sales@prakashbooks.com

facebook www.facebook.com/fingerprintpublishing
twitter www.twitter.com/FingerprintP
www.fingerprintpublishing.com

ISBN: 978 93 5440 549 5

Processed & printed in India

Dedicated to
My Mother Tongue

From the Heart

I am neither a litterateur nor a poet. At best you may call me an admirer of words.

For a long time, I have been in the process of accumulating my half-baked, part-delayed, part-scattered outpourings published at different times on different platforms. Finally, they have been strung together and compiled in this book.

I plead you to not equate my expression with my post or position, rather celebrate it for the merit of the thought and the emotion. The prose poetry in this book reflects my feelings, experienced from my little window of life. I don't claim these experiences to be extraordinary and there is a possibility that they have glimpses and echoes of all that I have read and heard in my growing-up years. You can describe them as operative influences on my life. These expressions were never meant for public scrutiny and therefore were not nurtured to perfection. I am also aware that not all my writings are sufficiently ripe as yet to be described as poetry and that is acceptable to me, because often it is the raw mango that leaves a lingering taste in the mouth.

My attraction for words stems out of my passion for reading. I am privileged to have interacted with the some of the best minds of Gujarati literature and fortunate that they included me in their creative journey of poetry readings and *kavi sammelans*. Suresh Dalal is one such evolved mind whom I admire and appreciate his quality to search for poetry everywhere and in everyone. There is a possibility that in my many interactions with him, he sensed the dormant writer within me and coerced me to open the floodgates of my heart. He emphasized that my writing, even though intended for personal expression, must not remain idle because who better than a Gujarati understands that all prime assets flourish only in circulation.

Thus began the process to find forsaken, forgotten countenance over the decades and build a new foundation. I searched old trunks, dusty diary pages, sepia-tinted lose sheets, some rolled, some folded inside forgotten books. I assembled crumpled folders and files, accumulated old and new writings, reread all, rewrote some, restructured a few and asked myself if the emotions still rankled. I was surprised that most of it still touched a raw nerve.

The exercise though daunting proved cathartic and as the rolls of paper—some joyous, some anguished scribbles—piled into a mound, I felt strangely satiated. Not because my writing was of merit but because I had accomplished the task I set out for, and the final outcome, good, bad, superior or mediocre, was secondary. The important point is that I own my outpourings. My writing reflects my churning, my vision, and my acute observations of people and life.

I invite my readers to come and rest beneath the shade of this full-bloomed tree and be a part of my journey.

Narendra Modi
Year 2007

Discovered in Translation

Those acquainted with Narendra Modi in his younger days reveal that he was in the habit of maintaining a diary, wherein he jotted his innermost thoughts and which is why he always carried a notebook and a pen with him everywhere he travelled.

Publishing these writings was never his intention, he says, which is why he did not labour over his expressions and yet his writings found an outlet.

It is always the first book that is difficult for any author because then, the author is unfamiliar with the process and therefore unsure of his decision to be published. When the author trusts the publisher, however, the process of publishing becomes enjoyable and perhaps that's what happened with Narendra Modi as well.

He entrusted his collection of writings to friend and publisher Suresh Dalal, who published *Aankh Aa Dhanya Chhe* in 2007. Almost fifteen years later, I stumbled upon the book and translated it as *Letters to Self*, a collection of sixty-seven poems written over a period of time. These are poems of progress, of despair, of quest, courage, and of compassion. He reflects over the mundane and the mysterious, mentions obscurities he wants to unravel. He is unafraid of being vulnerable, unafraid of expressing grief and when pain overwhelms, unafraid of shedding a solitary tear.

There are hurdles, there is restraint, he crusades against inequality and welcomes spring. He applauds the flight of the kites, is drawn to crowded, colourful fairs, he swirls with the garba, salutes the Narmada River, and mourns the Kargil soldiers!

The poems unfold like quick montages, varied images and moods, rushing past the lanes of time, resolutions, releases, mottos, mantras, and concerns for the body, soul and mind. Dreams, surprises, and decisions blossom, enlighten, and unfold. We see fleeting moments of hope, of loss, of fear, and of celebration in the poems. He expresses gratitude to life; gratitude for being born human with a free mind and to be able to feast on the beauties of nature.

The cosmos is a recurrent motif in his poetry. He is obsessed with nature and perennially in conversations with the mountains and the sea. He is enthralled by the sunlight, consumed by the starry night, the decorous moon is forever peeping from his phrases. He flirts with the celestial stars, caresses the clouds, lingers on the golden sand and the green meadows. The scented flowers with the dewdrops, the birds and the bees are his companions, he is forever in a dialogue with the trees, sensitive to their yearnings and indebted to their shade.

Narendra Modi creates powerful images with his rich vocabulary. What makes his writing different is his consistent emotional churning, his energy, and optimism. He expresses without filters, without reticence, and this intensity is infectious. His poems, prose, however you wish to describe his writings, strike a chord, awaken an old wound.

I am happy that Narendra Modi maintained a diary, happy that he did not polish his phrases, happy he displayed confidence to get them published because without them there would be no *Letters to Self*.

Bhawana Somaaya
2022

Contents

Gratitude

This planet is splendorous
And these eyes privileged
To feast on it

The sunlight drapes the lush, green grass
The sun rays, intense and unbearable
The universe is awe-inspiring
This planet is splendorous

The rainbow rotates, makes circles in the sky
Sketches and fills colours in the air
Is this a blessing from previous births?
Gratitude, deep heartfelt gratitude

The waves bounce and touch the sky
Wonder what lies in the embryo of the clouds?
The completeness is the beginning
This planet is splendorous

In a large fair of faces, I meet so many
I feel ill at ease
In their company
The disquietude
Is unsettling

And some of it, unimaginable

Gratitude, more gratitude
This planet is splendorous

All of a Sudden

On a black paper of darkness
I draw a pond
Over the pond stoops a branch
And on the branch, hums a bee

To diminish the darkness
I paint a luminous moon
Lend shades of blue to the breeze
As cool as the water in the pond

All of a sudden
The midsummer sun
Burns the paper
Turns it into ash
And the brush freezes in my hand

The frog croaks
Season of dreams
Or dreams of season
Everything disperses

Us

We are buddies for life
We are seekers of joy

No one dare stop us
No one dare daunt us
We are law unto ourselves

If we desire to, we fly away
Or dive into the sea
Emerge as the sun on the hills
And rise at midnight

Without thought
Without trepidation
Like gypsies
Driven in search of love

The wise call us crazy
They are right
We are not wrong

The vast sea overflows
We aren't bubbles
That burst

Forever without shores
We are tides amidst the ocean

Wail

Got to know about you
And it shattered my mountain heart
I saw you and
The moon shone in my eye
Sandalwood blossomed within me
We met, and every fibre of me
Exuded fragrance

But alas!
These mountains are melting
The perfume of sandalwood ignites me
And dreams turn to debris

Far away
The moon in my eye
Has returned to the horizon

Without you
There is no one
To row my boat
And take me to the shore
Will I ever find such a navigator?

Universe

Yesterday's path has come to an end
On its edge
Emerges the morning tree
On the branch of the breeze
Sways a flower of hope
The bird sings self-indulgently

I throw open all the windows
Identity has never appeared more exotic
My body, mind, and heart
Is a blessing from the Almighty
And the universe
Is clasped in my embrace

Today

This is it, that is it
It was here, it was there
Trouble troubles the mind
Prestige reduces to ruins

Also,
Why must we get entangled in the by-lanes
Like ghosts with extended shadows?

The past accompanied
By the ominous spirit
Is the haunting soul
Of our history

The soul is eternal
But even the immortal
Craves for present form

To become immortal tomorrow
Why engage in attachments
That betray our today?
Is this the purpose of life?

Dusk

Hour of dusk
I wander waif-like
Absorbing all I see
Like I am at a fair
In heightened sensitivity

I have nothing to seek
Nothing to lose
I live life like a celebration

My path is straight
No crowd
No baggage
Hour of dusk
I wander waif-like

No goals
No assets
I'm but human
Does it matter
Whether light comes from
The lamp or the lantern?

No sparkling chandeliers
Strung from the roof
Hour of dusk
I wander waif-like

Trouble

Once a beautiful, nubile river
Has scattered, turned ferocious
Like a tigress on the prowl

Lashed by heavy rains
She has overstepped
Shed all inhibitions

Lost control
Like a woman
Who has lost her mind,
She flows insanely

Probably unaware
How hard and cruel
Her water has transformed

It has drowned villages
Disrupted structures
Swept away corpses

So many lives lost
So many shrieks
So many cries for help
All dissolved into water
And flown away

The fury of nature
Exposes the cruelty
Of life-threatening sea

Ash

In hope of awareness
We dispel ignorance
In hope of illumination
We dispel the darkness

We have perforated the darkness
On the wheel of time
Now brightness has no barriers
The lamps sparkle today
Like multicoloured corals

Light, more light
Today, light is all around
In hope of brightness
We dispel the darkness

A thought, a movement
And a path to progress
A dogged intent to accomplish our goals
Has become our life-motto

We have locked all
Grievances
Light, more light
In hope of brightness
We dispel the darkness

Fame has no boundary
No preferences, no dislikes

Forgiveness fills this heart
Forever submitted to the Lord
Light, more light
In hope of brightness
We dispel the darkness

Loss of Warmth

In absence of compassion
The bravest is breathless
Then why does
Human abuse human?

Without water
The trees, the leaves, and the plants
Wither away
The cuckoo never sings
On an autumn tree

Why do humans
First support and then
Demolish each other?
In absence of compassion
The bravest is breathless

Devoid of love
Man is incomplete
Unfulfilled
He restores this loss
Linking
Stich by stitch
Moment to moment

With the silent sword
Of smile
He clips his tears
Without compassion
The bravest is breathless

Wake Up to Victory

The planet
Is going through
Arduous times

Let us unite
March together
Towards victory
Come,
Let us do it today

Let us bury
Old grievances
Let us blossom
As fragrant soil

Rise up, awake
Run, speed up
Holding hands
This isn't the time
For isolation

The planet
Is going through
Arduous times

The only way
To end human suffering
Unhappy existence
Is by firm determination

People appear different
But aren't really
Deep down we are
All the same

The planet
Is going through
Arduous times

So, emblazon the forehead
With the soil
This isn't the time
To sway on the swing
To take a backseat

March ahead
Find a new path
Pursue your dreams

This is not the hour
To indulge
The incapacitated
The incapable
This is the hour
For the courageous

Shriek so loud
That you burst the clouds
March like you walk into a fair

The planet
Is going through
Arduous times

Rise, Brave Heart

Covered in the quilt of slumber
The body sleeps
Wake up, brave heart
For the soul is now enlightened

It trails fire from the sky
Darts blazing arrows
Faces up to the ignited
Adversities
Strikes back as a shield

Listen to the wails of
Devi Kamakhya
Listen attentively
And awaken before it is late

Listen to the cries of Rukmini
And gallop to her aid
The way Dwarikadhish would
With the *Sudarshan Chakra*
In his hand
Become the flute
Spread the melody
If not now, it will be too late
Wake up, brave heart

Wake up and hasten
Before you are ravaged
In adulation
To ensure that
Humanity is never
Even remotely blemished

Dreams
Burn in fire
And crumble into ash
Ordinary lives
Turn ballot boxes
Into a death trap

The peak of Himalaya
Is on flames
Scamper to extinguish it
Save it, seek mercy
Wake up, brave heart

Assam trembles
With the shrieks of
Innocent killings
With fragile whimpers

Of beseeching corpses
Laid up on the pyre
Smouldering
Wake up, brave heart

It is not any one region
The soul of the nation
Is scathed
Wake up, brave heart
Abandon your patience
Before you get accustomed
To cowardice
Wake up, brave heart
Wake up
Before it is too late

Solitary Tear

Relationships blossom
Break and wither away
A solitary tear
Lingers in the eye

The frozen tear
Heavy as a rock
A deserted Sitar
With broken strings
Forgotten in a corner

Like a heatwave
That burns
But doesn't disappear
The solitary tear
Lingers in the eye

How long can we
Preserve
The broken pieces of crystal
The yearnings, the regrets
The appeals
Everything washes away
In flowing water
A solitary tear
Lingers in the eye

Melodious attachments
Now turn me restless
On a flower-festooned path
The thorns prick me
In my arid heart
There will never be a song

People Like That

They refrain to speak up
Where they ought to
And always speak
Where they should not
There are many like them
Surrounding me

Raise your voice
Speak what you must
Time to drop the façade
Of silence
Time to scathe
Time to startle

Never flatter the unworthy
Who refrain to express,
When they ought to
And always speak
What they shouldn't

To witness another condemn
And remain silent
Is a crime
To confess and accept mistake
Is a virtue
Worthy of forgiveness

In time of storm
The swaying trees
Lose decorum
From time immemorial
Nature does not lie

Celebration

Kite

Is a celebration of speed
My journey towards sunlight

Kite
Is my glory
My life string in my control

Feet entrenched on the ground
My kite soars high in the sky
Like a majestic bird

In a sky filled with kites
My kite unentwined
Is not enmeshed
On some branches
Of a tree

Kite
Is like my Gayatri Mantra
The affluent, the royal, and the poor
All love to assemble broken kites
It's a joy unusual, indescribable

The broken kite
Has experience of the horizon
Is acquainted with the speed
Of the winds

It has touched dizzying heights
And survived
Bearing testimony of its flight

Kite
Is my flight to sunlight
The string holds its breath
Its heart resides in the sky
I control the string of the kite
My Lord holds my string
The string desires the wind

Kite
Has unusual dreams
Different from humans
It ascends and ascends
Till it arrives
At the Lord's feet
The human sits in a corner
Untangling the knots

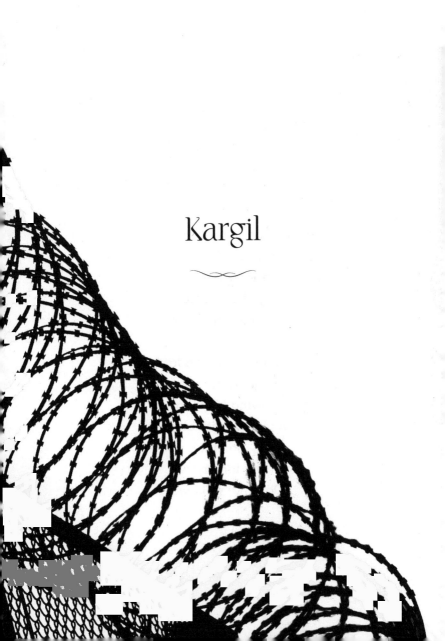

Kargil

Kargil
Had visited earlier too
Tiger Hill
Had seen it before
Then
I feasted on the pure
Tranquil majesty

Today,
Every peak reverberates
With bombs, rifles
On the snowcapped mountains
Spotted flames
Golden soldiers

Every soldier was a farmer
Here
Sowing his today
Watering with blood
So that
Our tomorrow
Does not wilt away

In the eyes of every soldier
I foraged
A million dreams
Clutching death
With their eyelashes

I observed the Lord of Death
Kiss the feet
Of these bravehearts
Saw their scalding bodies
Spread on slabs of ice
Trail into cold streams
And float away

As the nation bids farewell
To the patriot with
Sujjalam
Suffalam
The nation
The stream
Together sing
Vande Mataram
Vande Mataram

Verb

— ❦ —

Draw a circle of one word around me
Now make the circle into a square
Within the circular-square,
Place multicoloured marbles like words

Words of glass
Words of truth
Transparent words
Like teardrops
Or like full stops

Now sketch boundaries
Around the adjectives
Boundaries of Lakshman
Prestige of Ram
And play the cross and knots game
For as long as you want

And yes, place the adverbs
In the centre
And draw around them
An everlasting circle

Attitude

The crow bites the one who lies
Is that the reason we speak the truth?
Or because we relish truth
It is the only way of life?

If we refrain from truth
Then the crow will
Ambush the nightingale
Bite, break, and ravage it
Like it preys upon a stale fish

Headlines based on hearsay
Rise in the morning
Like black sunlight

In our path of truth
Towards revolution
All we encounter are
Allegations, accusations

Song of Speed

How long, can the dust from the cowsheds
Block the evening sunlight?
How long, can the piercing sunlight
Bite into the winter morning?
How long, can the afternoon sun
Stifle the dark streets?
Show some mercy, for God's sake

Stop sowing thorny shrubs in my arid fields
Stop, before they bleed some tender feet
Show some mercy, please

I want to sing a song for the reflection
Shining on the water pots
Carried by the *gopis*
A song for the daily wagers
Toiling in the tropical sun
A poem dedicated to their
Perspiration
Sparkling like dewdrops in the sun

I want to separate the dust
Raised by the tender feet
Walking barefoot on the field
From the dust of the cowsheds

I want to create a gallery of this dust
I want to sketch a portrait of the speed
Create a painting of progress
Because this picture is pigmented

The stain
Another name for speed, for progress
Is but a result
Of our misdeeds
Dust raised by our tender feet
Soiled with our own blood
And therefore, the blemish
The only indicator
Of our speed, our progress

Now
Stop disguising the blemish
I want to sing a song for the blazing sun
Sparkle energy into the tender feet again
Wait and watch
The new album will be devoid of the stain

But alas . . .
Before that
So many tender feet soaked in blood

Have been sacrificed
Into the burning of the thorny shrubs

And therefore, I plead
Let us stop growing destructive shrubs
I want to sing a song of movement
I want to sing a song of progress

Garbo

Garbo

Belongs to the one who sings it,
also to the one who echoes
Garbo is the pride of Gujarat,
also the glory of Gujarat

It belongs to the one who swirls to it,
also to the one who twirls to it
Garbo is the pride of Gujarat,
also the glory of Gujarat

It is the sun and the moonlight,
and also the changing season
Garbo is the pride of Gujarat,
also the glory of Gujarat

It is the dawn and also the dusk
Garbo is the pride of Gujarat,
also the glory of Gujarat

Garbo is tradition and also the cosmos
It is the flute and also the peacock feather

Garbo is a thought and also an affirmation
It belongs to the brave and also to the affluent

Garbo is body and also the soul
It is tranquillity and also contentment

Garbo is Sati and also progression
It is a continuity of women power

Garbo is truth, it is everlasting
Like the vermillion of the mother Goddess
Garbo is splendorous

In the Song

A song travels
Within the feather of a bird
A song
Where the nightingale speaks
And also sings

One wing of the bird
Is linked to the earth
The other wing,
Measures the sky

On my paper
I draw an orange sun
Also, a full moon
On my paper blooms a tree
On the tree a green leaf
Smiles

Like a stream
Moistening memories
Of loved ones
Parked far away

On one side, rests the desert
On the other, the sea
On the third,
The flow of the river

The heart is thirsty
For the Lord
And try as I would
I cannot camouflage it

I trudge holding
The horizon in my eyes
Seated on the ground

Tuberoses

Deep, dark manhole
And recurrent mayhem around it

I want to be the bridge
That binds intentions to affection
If everyone is in harmony
It is a celebration

If not, no point hanging out
In a wasteland
It is worthwhile
To bloom like a rose

All hurdles are surmounted
We have discovered a tuberose

Pride

I'm forever proud that I'm human
That I'm Hindu
That I'm privileged to be a drop
In this vast ocean

I will eliminate none
I will include all
I relish human company
Blossom in their shower of warmth

Narmada flows in my veins
A dewdrop on a flower
I'm forever proud that I'm human
That I'm Hindu

The eyes appear small
But the vision is clairvoyant
With collective efforts
It is possible
To usher unity in diversity

Sun, clouds, stars and other planets
Are speckles in my sky
I'm forever proud that I'm human
That I'm Hindu

Release

Detach from the body
From affection
Detach from material joys
And all its trappings

Demolish the forts
Destroy the cage
Break free
From velvet dreams

Wandering night
Wastrel night
Blabbering night
Lonely night

Desert the words
Their implications
Break the foundations
Of speculations

If no one is with you
Walk alone
If someone accompanies
Not a problem

Break free from the rigmarole
Accept, embrace a new path

Unknown

I like the sun
It firmly holds the reins
Of all its seven horses

One has never known
Of him ever striking
A single horse

And yet,
The rays of the sun
The speed
Its direction
Is aimed at the well-being
Always passionate

Under the Umbrella

If successful, I am the cause of envy
If failure, I am subject to pity

I cross the boundary of both
To wait at a third corner

Not the kind to court cowardice
And uncaring of the incapacitated

I have lived life wholeheartedly
I yearn for the end

In the protection of my Lord
I learn every day
I am a student

If successful, I am the cause of envy
If failure, I am subject to pity

The salty ocean of criticism
Or the honey-sweet praises
Are both, futile fleeting shades

What matters is that
You preserve and protect
Your own story

I pray
That when time beckons
On the battlefield
I don't waver
I don't quaver

If successful, I am the cause of envy
If failure, I am subject to pity.

Call of the Spring

End of the beginning
Or beginning of the end
In the heart of the autumn
Sings the cuckoo
At sixteen
It is forever spring
Over whom does the flower
Shower its blossom?

They appear deprived
But are prosperous
In the heart of the autumn
Sings the cuckoo

Today
The desert blooms
Like a wedding
The trees radiate
Like stars

The sages arrive
To offer blessings
In the heart of the autumn
Sings the cuckoo.

It Is Up to You

You can address the water
As a stone
Or the other way round
You can describe the cloud
as a crease in the sky
Or a lotus
As a thorny bush
It does not matter

Can you define propaganda
As truth?
Can day be mistaken
For the night?
Or autumn be confused
With the spring?
Can the sea be
Introduced as the desert?
Or life be mixed up
For death?

Words you choose
Reflect your character
Fact is
Nature is constant
Robust and rooted

Beyond the Image

I exist in my picture
And I don't
I exist in my poster
And I don't
No oppositions
No contradictions

The image is not like
The soul
It drenches with water
Burns with fire
And when it burns
Or drenches
I remain unaffected

Don't search for me
In my picture or poster
Don't make futile efforts
I am secure
In my self-confidence
My words, my conduct
And my Karma.

Judge me by my work
My work is my life

Life disciplined
Like the verses
Rhythmic
Melodious

I have been groomed
In the cradle
And perfected
As I turned older

For all of you
The wail and the pathos
Is an outburst of unfiltered affection

Don't search for me
In the frame
Hunt for me in earnestness
You will find me dwelling
In productive plans
Of the universe

Recognize me by my tone
My echo
You will find your reflection
In my eyes

Scene

In a forest filled with trees
I sit beneath one
The green grass swings me
In the cloud
Butterflies flap their wings
The bee hovers over the flower
And the flower submits

Scenes alter
Eyes meet
Dusk falls
And within me awakens
A full-blown tree

In the darkness
Stars blossom like flowers
Wearing wings
Borrowed from the butterflies
I float in the sky

Like a buzzing firefly
Trickling a trail of light
Spreading a fragrant tune
I spread the bloom of the
Cosmos
The green grass rocks my heart
High into the sky

Body and Mind

The body follows its rhythm
The mind chases its path
In a garden of letters
I stare at Sita Ram

The Veena sings without voice
Evokes a gentle beat
This heart chants
Your one exquisite name

The body follows its rhythm
The mind chases its path

In my heart, body, and mind
Springs a high tide of love
As my life flows and floats
In my eyes

My one Ayodhya
And one Raghupati Rajaram
The body follows its rhythm
The mind chases its path

Narmada

Narmada is not just a river
She is meditation
She is devotion

Narmada is not a line on the map
She is the fate of Gujarat
She is the destiny of people

If you contaminate Narmada
Or dare to soil her pure water
Beware of Sant Kabir

Narmada belongs to Gandhiji
To Narmad and to Munshiji
It is the dream street of Sardar
Narmada is the joy of Gujarat

Narmada is tradition
A wish-fulfilling Goddess

Narmada is not just a river
She is meditation
She is devotion

Innocent

Who cares about destiny?
I am up for challenges

I don't borrow light
I am the burning lantern

Not dependent on outside glitter
I am content with my own shine

The whirlpool dispels darkness
The spark from its current
Is invigorating

I am not attracted to the mist
I am open-hearted and guileless

Who cares about destiny?
I am up for challenges

I am not drawn to horoscopes
I don't bow to celestial stars
Cowards don't stake life
On the chessboard

I am my legacy
I am my heir

Who cares about destiny?
I am up for challenges

Challenge

There is a sound to the earth
A sound to the sky
And a destination for the road
I challenge, I beseech

Spread out in a habitat
Human has transformed into
A demon

The cacophony has turned
The habitat
Into a riot

There are walls of pride
And dreams have turned to debris
I challenge, I beseech

Equality is an illusion
Unity, trampled upon
The doors and the door frames
Are scattered helter-skelter
Fallen into ditches

Tears flow uncontrolled
Surrounding the darkness
I challenge, I beseech

The body is famished
The mind is broken
And people wounded
By each other

Time to drop pomposity
Time to unite as a tribe

There is fire in the eyes
To shatter the walls
I challenge, I beseech

Unearth the dreams beneath the ruins
They are necessities of life

Break away from the past
Fling open your hearts
Broaden your horizon
Uplift the drowned

Holding each other's hand
Let us brighten our lives
I challenge, I beseech

Butterfly

It sits on a flower then flies away
The butterfly immerses into
The colours again

In a perfumed pond nearby
The butterfly floats like a boat
A tender sun rises like joy
It sits on a flower then flies away

Life is wondrous
Because of
The flurry of activity
People enter and exit
And memories linger on

A web created is never easily broken
The butterfly immerses into colours again

Introduction

Time alters perceptions
It morphs introductions
I am the honey bee
Sun of winter morning
Inside, summer time

Unlike the fly I don't park
Here, there, everywhere
I sit beside the flower
And inhale its aroma

Dressed in pink petals
I flutter in the cool breeze

Time alters perceptions
It morphs introductions
I am the honey bee

Meadows reverberate a melody
And a spray of colours
Instils joy

I decline the path defined
Follow my own rules

On the surface
I appear a vagabond

But I am the emperor
Of my heart

Time alters perceptions
It morphs introductions
I am the honey bee

At times
The stone hits you
At times
You hit the stone
And stumble
The difference
Is all in the mind

From the stone
I sculpt the steps
A staircase
That ascends me to heights

Almighty is with me
And with everyone
I am companion to all

Time alters perceptions
It morphs introductions
I am the honey bee

Transparent

I am not in favour of
Dark, mysterious silence
I am not in favour of
Shielding heinous crimes

I prefer to be transparent
Like the water
I celebrate
The tranquil flow

I don't chase mirages
I break illusions
Of frogs fantasizing
Paradise within puddles

There is no shame
In defying injustice
And bowing to justice

I am not in favour of
Dark, mysterious silence
I am not in favour of
Shielding heinous crimes

Waiting

The sun rises like a rock
In the sky
Spreads like a tattered cloth
Over the day
The dry wind
Acts rather strange
With the tree

The afternoon coughs
Incessantly
Like a long, ailing patient
And the evening
Powerlessly descends
Dissolves into darkness
Black as the ditch

The sunflower
Waits all night
For the morning sun
Waits
For the sun to bloom
Like a flower

Mercy of God

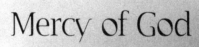

Oh Lord
If I displease myself
Or the world
I will bear with it
But it is unacceptable
That I will ever let you down

It is your grace
That transforms the thorns into flowers
You protect me from the torrential rains
With sunshine

Seasons come and seasons go
It is your presence that makes
This heart
Forever feel like spring

Your generosity is boundless
And sometimes, I question myself
And you:
What do I do or not do
That will make you joyous?

Trials

∽◦∽

I will not do anything
That will make me
Hang my head in shame

I will stand sturdy
Like the mountain
And flow pristine
Like the river

These are not
Decorative words
Rather expressions
From deep within
I love this planet
Celebrate its silence
With a song

In the tune of tradition
Echoes a trapped century
I will never do anything
That will make me
Hang my head in shame

Every deed I enact
Has blessings of the Lord
One who does no wrong
Says the voice within
Has nothing to fear

My conduct
Reflects my words
And this remains unchanged
I will not do anything
That makes me hang
My head in shame

Prayer

Crowd or funfairs
Friends or well-wishers
I welcome all
In my abode
The message outside my door
Reads:
Truth is welcome
Never mind that it is up-close
Never mind that it is tilted

The stench of the manure
Is more precious
Then the scent
Of the meadows
I have the competence
To search for truth
In opposition

I have the fortitude
To dust off the rumours
You cannot live life
Based on the grapevine

I have the forbearance
To seek truth
Between the extremes

Everyone has a different truth
And this is possible
I will stay as close as possible
To my truth

Truth for me is sunlight
My guiding light
Like Gayatri Mantra
And it remains so
Every moment
Is my prayer

Love

My love is like the water chain
Unbinding
I disapprove of promises
In relationships
They turn me restless

Like dewdrops frozen all night
My love isn't easy to capture

The sunlight cannot be grasped
In a fist
And the blowing wind
Isn't comfortable
In a cage
My carefree, cloud-like love
Cannot be seized

Mist appears and disappears
But cannot fade out sunlight

My love cannot be held
Nor strung like beads
It paddles
Like the floating swan

My love is like the water chain
Unbinding

Pressure

Υes
I attempted to capture
The high mountains
But collected merely rocks

Yes
I attempted to occupy
The blossoming gardens
But encountered merely thorns
Beneath my feet

Yes
For centuries I craved
To retain the river
But managed to hold mere bubbles
In my palms

Yes
The blazing sun
Forever stayed far away
My pictures of it captured
Merely the shadow

Yes
I attempted to inherit the moon
And lost sight of the horizon

Is that the reason
A wave rolled over to the shore
And shed a quiet tear?

Midnight

The nightingale sings at midnight
Opens her heart, shares secrets
How does one admonish
The nightingale?

How does one explain
That she must not spill over
Intimate moments
She must not spread herself
Like the waves
Indiscriminately
She must not scatter her feelings
Loosely
She must not measure emotions
On a scale
How does one admonish
The nightingale?

How does one explain
That our pain is private
And there's not a soul
Around
That can be trusted!

Why does she thump
The fastened doors?
Why does she rummage
In mirages?
How does one admonish
The nightingale?

My Heart

The heart is blistered
The body on flames
I stand amidst a desert
Searching
In a fragrant garden

I have met the cheerful
Acquainted with the
Anguished
Observed the ailing
Watched the feasting

One who is detached
Is devoid of malaise
Like a synchronized
Instrument
Always in perfect tune

I console my heart
Plead it to awaken
Before it is too late

I have cleared the thorns
Spread a carpet of flowers
Sown rainbows
On a desolate land

I seek hard work
Forever to embellish
In perspiration

Blend Wholeheartedly

The noisy sea
Striving to embrace
The sky
Is my inspiration
The reason
Of my strength
My youthfulness

It plays the *Shehnai*
And raises slogans
As well
Points to the peaks
Of the mountains

She is irreverent
Towards the shores
But if we depict
Courage
The sea is ready
To fling flower of foam
On our palms

The flower emanates
The aroma of the
Waves

The spillover recounts
The river's pain of parting
Once submerged into the sea
The river can never be
Separated

I can stand rock-steady
Like a mountain
And also overflow
Like the sea

You can carve me
You can scrape me
Or like water
You can imprint on me

Hold me
Chisel me
In compassion
With the hammer of love

The wall of the horizon
The roof of the sky
People, more people
Scenic beauty
Shape of my home
Vigour of my mind
The entire universe

Mantra

Full moon night, barren desert
The sand sparkles like gold dust
The splendorous moment
Is forever connected with eternity

In the flow of life
Moments come
Moments go
Flowing water
Streaming light
Passing breeze
Fragrant flowers
Burning lamp
I sense it all

But this life
That comes and goes
I'm unaware of its whereabouts
Never inquired its address

Last evening,
Life could have paused
It is possible to live moments
Gone past
It is possible to light a lamp

Of hope
It is possible for darkness
To kiss the light
It is possible to seize a moment
Of the flowing life

So many moments
I bumped into life briefly
So many moments
I celebrated life
Walking helter-skelter
I paused for a while

Every breath is savoury
Every expression is love
Has memories of
The evening gone by
Tears interrupted
Hope to brim over
Dormant dreams
Hold a new dawn

In a mechanical life
I have discovered
An unknown mantra
Of utmost beauty

Mother, Give Me Strength

I sit cocooned in your heart
Shower me with blessings
Dear mother

Bless me with sanctity
Bless me with strength
Bless me with truth

My only plea
Is that at every step
I receive
Your love
Your solace

O mother shower me with sanctity
Shower me with strength
I sit cocooned in your heart

I have abandoned rage
Settled for abstinence
No quest for flowers
No residue of fragrance

Your presence exudes
So many hues

But they appear all distant
Far from intimate

The only one to
Offer compassion
Is you, mother!
Dear mother
Bless me with sanctity
Bless me with strength

My path is brave
Your affection endless
My life is your love
My life is your light
Ever heard of the ocean sob?
Then why must we complain?
Dear mother,
Bless me with sanctity
Bless me with strength

The orchards and the meadows
Will one day, turn arid
The blossoming flowers
Will wilt away
The gardener will waver
In his passion too
At that time, dear mother

Soak the soil in your tears
Shut your lids to all drawbacks.
String a garland of flowers
So unique
It radiates with divinity
Dear mother
Bless me with sanctity
Bless me with strength

Attachment

I am drawn to the blank paper
When you look into its heart
The blank paper hides many faces

Face of the cloud
And when the cloud bursts
Lush green grass

Somewhere I notice
The trees and the hills
And the eyes can hear
The breath of the breeze

Nobody is a stranger
No one unfamiliar
We are all bonded
In silence

The bee, the butterfly
And the unusual fireflies
Together, build a nest

When I inhale the paper
I smell the moistness
Of the first rain

I have discovered
A tender shade
I wrap myself
In unknown shadows

I am drawn to the blank paper
When you look into its heart
The blank paper hides many faces

Mingle in the Fair

To interpret the crowd in a fair
Is my motto, my joy;

Man loiters in a fair
Meeting, smiling
Enjoying himself

I endorse affirmation
I delete all doubts
Lend support
To a crumbling
Foundation

Behind man is the Almighty
I possess the flute
And the *Shiv Dhanush*

Between the God and the devil
I remain human
And to be human
Is by no means ordinary

To experience paradise
On this planet
Is my only plea

Let the crowd loiter
Let the people mingle, feel free

Journey

I can travel far, far away
Into my past
And can recognize every face
Distinctly

There's no strain in recalling
These memories
I see them clearly
And comprehend them

Nothing is out of order
The fact of the matter is

Those with whom
You have suffered
Are unforgettable

And the anguish
Endured together
Eventually,
Transcends into a journey

I can travel far, far away
Into my past

Mystery

~~~~

I don't want to see
The tall, rigid trees
Shrouded in black robes
I want to see them
In bright sunlight
Surrounded by
Blossoming flowers
Chirping birds

The cheer of
The morning trees
The youthful ecstasy
Of the afternoon trees
And the quiet wisdom
Of the evening trees
I want to revel in them all
Imprint the memories
Deep inside my heart

Trees are indicators
Of my soul
The burning afternoon breath
Seeks refuge in my shadow

Blessed by the winds
I relish the feeble drizzle
Of raindrops

Trees: the root of my existence
Is my mystery

Farewell Friend

In the fluorescent of the moonlight
Falls the shadow of the eclipse
Before the dreams can bloom
Footsteps of autumn intervene

The night rises at noon
Darkness spreads over the eyes
Without Ramesh Parekh
My heart sinks
Time has turned devilish
And mute tears hurt deep

I describe Ramesh's writing as scriptures
And with fond memories address
Amreli
As the land of poetry
Who do I share my wounds with?

In eyes without spectacles
I see Ramesh everywhere

Aided by words
I want to make it to the poetry post
Have fitted Ramesh Parekh's picture
Back into the frame

Towards My Goal

In pursuit of my goal
I lose myself
I race, I skip, and at times
Stumble too
On the blood-soaked path
But continue to trudge
Stare at the blood-stained feet
With a tear and a smile

On the pyres of the departed
The sunlight bounces
The lustre
Pales my smile
Fades their flames
And that's when
My ego drops
The speed escalates
And the goal approaches closer

Vande Mataram

Vande Mataram
Is not a song
It is our glory
Our offering
To our independence
The song arouses
National pride

The Republic Day
Celebrates
The forever beating heart
Pulse of progress
Our unusual introduction

1857 is a cluster of light
Truth soars
And the blood flow
Persists

Vande Mataram
Is not a word
It is a mantra
The energy
The heartbeat
Of our freedom
Our royal path
To progress
Our commitment
To our nation
Every morning
Of my public life
Is a call
Of enlightenment
Vande Mataram

Difficult and Strange

Is it possible,
That the moon rises
And the sea doesn't overflow?

Is it possible,
That the sun shines
And the sunflower doesn't blossom?

Is it possible,
That the river will decline to unite with the sea?

Is it possible,
That the flower blooms
And the moth is not attracted?

Is it possible,
That the bells will clang
And the temple doors will not open?

Is it possible,
That the lamps are lit
And the shrine doesn't sparkle?

Is it possible then?
That love can be so difficult and so strange?

Dauntless Dawn

The night of gloom
Has descended
Victory awakens at dawn
Celebrate this dawn
Celebrate the bright
Tomorrow
Dark, ominous walls
Have crumbled
A courageous dawn
Today awakens

Like soldiers riding
The war-chariots
Let us together pledge
To incorporate all
And abandon vested interests
The flower
And the scent of the flower
Await
A courageous dawn
Today awakens

There's no chronicle of pain
No regrets, no mourning
The storm has passed

The boundary of the
Expansive sky has extended
All troubles have dispelled
And flower petals
Strewn on the floor
A courageous dawn
Today awakens

Joy springs unbridled
Perfumed dreams
Uncensored
When you trust the Lord
With your heart
There is no reason
For bitterness
A courageous dawn
Today awakens

Let Pain Be Expressed

Let pain be expressed
Let the tears flow
Let flowers droop
Let them roll into dust
And fade

Dreams are drenched
Without reason, all knotted
Allow the frosted tear
Halted at the corner of the eye
To watch intently
Like the Jacobine Cuckoo
Let pain be expressed
Let the tears flow

Moments spill over
Expectations blush
Unknown hearts
Somewhere bounce
Let the swan gently float
In the lake of my eyes
Let pain be expressed
Let the tears flow

Dreams of joy and sorrow
Are fleeting attachments
I have shielded myself
In a quilt of clouds
Allow the aggregated clouds
To burst, my beloved
Urge the showers to fall
Uninhibitedly
Let pain be expressed
Let the tears flow

Words

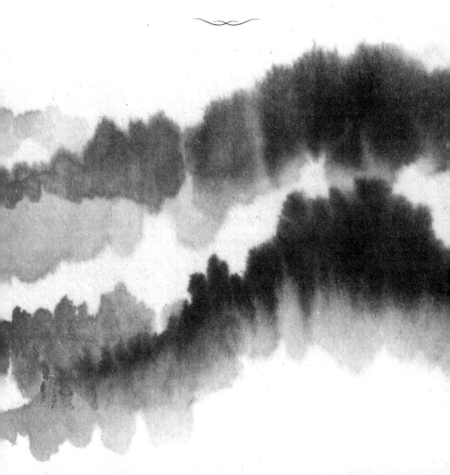

My words, like rocks
Flowing into the
Singing water
Create new sound
A unique language
Connecting us

Together
But in different company
We pine for
An everlasting shadow

I am the emperor of stories
And you,
The queen of epic

The river has two shores
One belongs to you
The other is for me
Time moves on
Like a mendicant
Without a break
He is well versed
With the story
And still intrigued

Eternal Season

Everyday meetings, large crowds
Cluster of cameramen, blinding lights
Deafening microphones
I am not acquainted to all this, as yet
Thank God

I am still bewildered
From where the words flow
Sometimes for injustice
I raise my voice
Sometimes gentle words
Flow like a tranquil sea

Sometimes like spring
Words spread cheer
On their own
Adorn costumes of meaning
And ride like a caravan
As I stare
At its galloping speed

Amidst all these
Innumerable words
I guard my solitude
Treasure the embryo of silence
And celebrate an eternal season

Seeds of Dreams

I call a stone a stone
And water as water

I am pragmatic
I watch the horizon
I'm attracted to the rainbow
But I don't build my home
On a rainbow

Like the rainbow
I have colourful dreams
Not romantic
More meditative
Churned out of my suffering

You may have dreams too
Or maybe not
But I sow seeds of dreams
In my garden
I toil and till the land
Then wait in anticipation
For the sprout to blossom
Into a tree
Spread into branches
Far and wide

On the tree
The birds build nests
And slowly touch the sky
When the birds sing
The rivers entwine
And the divine music
Reverberates

Amalgamation

To the night born
Out of the womb of darkness
I whisper:
Come, sit beside me
I'm overflowing with love for you
I haven't stopped smiling
Since your arrival
I am not certain
Between the two of us
Who nurtures the other?
But this much I understand
That together
We bloom, turn fragrant like
Flowers
Indifferent to the thorns

On the branch of the day
It's not only the flowers that bloom
The birds sing
And the song spreads fragrance
The song has no shape
Nor does fragrance
But both travel
And the amalgamation
Of their position and movement
Is my meditation

Come, let us together
Embrace the showered blessings
And live wholeheartedly
For as long as we can

Facing the Storm

Generosity
Liveliness
Are oars
Of my life
Galaxy of stars
The moon
In the sky
My mentors

The celestial stars
Are unaware of
The crack inside the sea
Unaware of the country
Divided by Partition
For the sea without walls
It makes no difference
Which side is Hindustan?
And which is Pakistan?
They trespass every day
And are punished every day

No one comes to bail them out
No one announces release orders
But
The heart burns for the nation
Scarlet angry flames in the sea

Pledge

Sometimes, the sun rises
Streaming fireballs
Burning me on a hot, hot day
In a sky engulfed in flames
I search for a tranquil base
To escape the scorching rays
I weave a maze of shadow play
In a caravan of thoughts
I arrive at an extraordinary
Decision

The shine of a pledge
Its energy
Its enthusiasm
Its affection
Its company
The rising evening
The cows coming home
Are symbols of prosperity
Signs of affluence
Human body is not dependent
And helplessness not part
Of my character

Memory

Faded sepia memories
Venture out to embrace
The past
The dense fog cannot be
Penetrated
Darkness cannot be dispelled

Memory crumbles like dry leaf
From a tree
What does it indicate,
When memory dims away?
What does it mean to bottle up memory?
What does it indicate of its potency?

In memory, deserts overflow
Like sea in the midsummer
Memory has no nails
But it scratches and wounds
Blow out all the lamps of memory
Clip off its wings
Pull out its nails
It is impossible to drag memory out
So burst her eyes
And cut off her tongue
But her lips cannot be sewed

Because
Memory never suffers a blackout
It banishes darkness
Memory chokes my throat
Wrecks my life

Memory has many colours, many shades
It is sunlight, also shade
It is devoid of the sound of footsteps
It is devoid of footprints as well
Memory has no ascent, no descent

Should memory be called death?
Should it be described as refuge?
Memory has no form
And no dwelling place
Memory is a flowing stream
It is memory that keeps our life afloat

Hindu Hindu Mantra

Here, there, everywhere
Hindu Hindu is a mantra
Bindu Bindu is a mantra
Sindhu Sindhu is a mantra

This mantra is as precious as a pearl
Like a luminous light in darkness
We will spread light
We will spread light in the world

We will eradicate the divide between
The fortunate and the deprived
We will demolish self
And make society prosper
We will inspire a song of perseverance
We will build a temple within the heart
And spread enlightenment
We will spread light

There will be no enemies
All will be friends
We will evolve a persona
That will diffuse all conflicts
We will initiate new dialogue
We will spread light

Food, clothing, tradition, facility
Will be easily accessible
The grass will be lush green
And the sky filled with stars

Unity
Equality
Compassion
Will be preserved with effort and care
We will spread light
We will spread light in the world

Eleventh Direction

Fearless mind
A tuneful song
Everlasting
Love in the heart
A smile like a dream
A cheerful wind
A scented sky
It's the seeker who makes
Every moment precious

The earth
Is forever
Affectionate
Fragrant
The Lord, my beloved
I stare at unblinking
There is no past
Nothing unknown
Just immortal
Moments

No rituals
No ceremonies
Just quietude
Reflected
On my face

Far away,
From ten directions
A song plays quietly
In the eleventh direction

One who loves my country
is my God.

Acknowledgments

I thank Image Publishers Pvt. Ltd., Mumbai, Ahmedabad, for publishing Shri Narendra Modi's Gujarati book *Aankh Aa Dhanya Chhe* from which I was able to translate *Letters to Self* for English readers.

Appreciate Bhakti Desai Shetty for her valuable time and feedback.

Thanks to the entire team of Fingerprint! Publishing.

Bhawana Somaaya has been a film critic for more than forty years and has contributed columns to various publications. She is the former editor of *Screen* and has authored several books on cinema that include biographies of Hema Malini and Amitabh Bachchan. Her books are a point of reference for students studying cinema at Whistling Woods, Manipal University, and JNU, Delhi.

She has served on the Advisory Panel of CBFC India, and also the Governing Council FTII, Pune, and is the entertainment editor at 92.7 Big FM radio channel.

In 2008, she released *Keshava: A Magnificent Obsession*, and *Letters to Mother* which is an English translation of the Prime Minister of India's Gujarati book *Saakshi Bhaav*, published in 2020. *Letters to Self* is a translation of Shri Narendra Modi's book *Aankh Aa Dhanya Chhe*.

Bhawana Somaaya was conferred with Padma Shri in 2017 and with an honorary doctorate by Jagran Lake City University in 2021.